MADRID

THE CITY AT A GLA

C000065904

Cuatro Torres
Yup, four towers. Way talle
not just in Madrid, but the
See p015

Puerta de Europa
The symmetry and engineering feats of this
drunk-looking duo remain mighty impressive.
See p074

Torre de Madrid
One of Europe's tallest buildings in 1957 when
it topped out at 142m, the Otamendi brothers'
mixed-use modernist giant is back in fashion.
See p018

Edificio España
The up-and-down (and up again) tale of this
heavyweight sums up the city's last 65 years.
See p011

Palacio Real
On a strategic vantage point since medieval
times, Spain's neoclassical palace, designed by
Italy's best architects, was completed in 1751.
See p009

Torre Europa
Part of a cluster of 1980s high-rises (see p014)
that broke the city mould, Europa continues to
do so, thanks to its 'smart' conversion.
Paseo de la Castellana 95

Museo de las Colecciones Reales
Impressively dug mostly below the cathedral,
the museum will display the nation's treasures.
See p078

Catedral de la Almudena
The first stone was laid in 1883 but it was only
consecrated in 1993 (still not quite finished).
Calle de Bailén 10

INTRODUCTION
THE CHANGING FACE OF THE URBAN SCENE

In the noughties, Madrid went through a cycle of economic growth, urban expansion and creative excitement not seen since La Movida Madrileña in the 1980s. Whereas Barcelona went global when it hosted the 1992 Olympics and has since become saturated with EU émigrés, giving it a superficial veneer of glamour, Madrid's allure runs deeper and its development has been far more organic.

The Euro debt crisis and rising unemployment have been hard on its residents, but as they became selective in their spending, the city reinvented itself. Despite the country's recent political scandals, the mayor of Madrid, Manuela Carmena, has been a force for good since 2015. The arts movement has continued to evolve and thrive (see p056), as has the social scene. And for all the establishments that have pulled down their shutters for the last time, there is no lack of hip restaurants, bars and clubs ready and willing to replace them. Now, as ever, the city's kicking nightlife, immortalised by film director Pedro Almodóvar, suits all budgets and persuasions.

And it is this indomitable spirit, together with the capital's many highbrow pleasures (see p024) – and, yes, low prices – that pull in tourists in droves (up 15.8 per cent in 2017 from the previous year). For locals, the flipside of designer digs opening in every district has been a spike in rents. However, this has never been a city that feels as if its culture is being stifled by a foreign invasion. For behind the imperial facade of this vibrant metropolis is the very soul of Spain.

ESSENTIAL INFO

FACTS, FIGURES AND USEFUL ADDRESSES

TOURIST OFFICE
Centro de Turismo
Plaza Mayor 27
T 91 454 4410
www.esmadrid.es

TRANSPORT
Airport transfer to city centre
Metro trains depart regularly from 6.05am
to 1.30am. It takes around 20 minutes to
Nuevos Ministerios, from where you can
connect to central Madrid
Car hire
Avis
T 90 220 0162
Metro
Trains run from 6am to 2am
www.metromadrid.es
Taxi
Radio Taxi Gremial
T 91 447 5180
Travel card
A three-day Abono Turístico de Transporte
pass costs €18.40

EMERGENCY SERVICES
Emergencies
T 112
24-hour pharmacy
Farmacia Goya 89
Calle Goya 89
T 91 435 4958

EMBASSIES
British Embassy
Paseo de la Castellana 259d
T 91 714 6300
www.gov.uk/world/spain
US Embassy
Calle de Serrano 75
T 91 587 2200
es.usembassy.gov

POSTAL SERVICES
Post office
Paseo del Prado 1
T 91 523 0694
UPS
T 90 288 8820

BOOKS
Fortunata and Jacinta by
Benito Pérez Galdós (Penguin)
**Madrid and the Prado:
Art and Architecture** by
Barbara Borngässer (Ullman)
Madrid: Architectural Guide by Juan
Valle Robles and Irene Valle Robles (DOM)
**Remaking Madrid: Culture, Politics,
and Identity After Franco** by
Hamilton M Stapell (Palgrave Macmillan)

WEBSITES
Art
www.madridstreetartproject.com
Newspaper
www.elpais.com

EVENTS
ARCO
www.ifema.es/arcomadrid_06
Estampa Contemporary Art Fair
www.estampa.org

COST OF LIVING
Taxi from Barajas Airport to Centro
€30
Cappuccino
€1.50
Packet of cigarettes
€5
Daily newspaper
€1.50
Bottle of champagne
€50

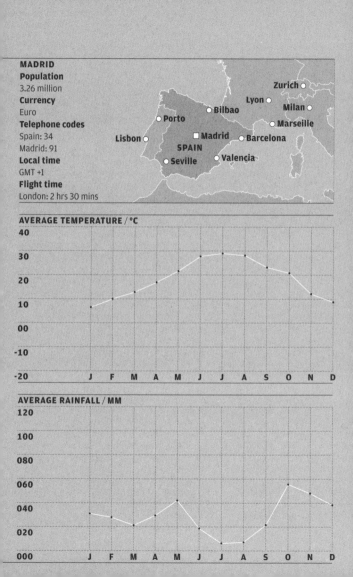

MADRID
Population
3.26 million
Currency
Euro
Telephone codes
Spain: 34
Madrid: 91
Local time
GMT +1
Flight time
London: 2 hrs 30 mins

Zurich
Lyon
Milan
Bilbao
Porto
Marseille
Lisbon
Madrid
Barcelona
SPAIN
Valencia
Seville

AVERAGE TEMPERATURE / °C

40												
30												
20												
10												
00												
-10												
-20	J	F	M	A	M	J	J	A	S	O	N	D

AVERAGE RAINFALL / MM

120												
100												
080												
060												
040												
020												
000	J	F	M	A	M	J	J	A	S	O	N	D

NEIGHBOURHOODS

THE AREAS YOU NEED TO KNOW AND WHY

To help you navigate the city, we've chosen the most interesting districts (see below and the map inside the back cover) and colour-coded our featured venues, according to their location; those venues that are outside these areas are not coloured.

SALAMANCA

Its elegant avenues are home to the upper classes (known as *pijos*). Glittery flagships present luxe global brands and high-end local designers, and the neo-Mudéjar HQ of newspaper *ABC* is now a mall. Upmarket restaurants like Santerra (General Pardiñas 56, T 91 401 3580) cater to the in-crowd.

CASTELLANA

Paseo de la Castellana, the city's financial centre, is a multi-lane boulevard lined with skyscrapers (see p015). But most visitors come here to see the Galácticos play at the Bernabéu (Avenida de Concha Espina 1, T 91 398 4300). Nearby, check out Joan Miró's mural on the Palacio de Congresos (No 99).

MADRID RÍO

The rebirth of the once-grimy Manzanares river has been a proper success. The banks have now been landscaped, and it attracts joggers, skaters and families having picnics. Get your culture fix at Matadero (see p028) and sample the Basque cuisine at Latxaska Etxea (Paseo del Molino 8, T 91 527 1067).

CHUECA/MALASAÑA/CONDE DUQUE

Madrid's gay hub, Chueca has become a playground for all the city's youth, packed with chic eateries (see p050), boutiques, funky bars and clubs. La Movida Madrileña spewed out of Malasaña in the 1980s, and it remains a mecca for alternative lifestyles. Conde Duque is noted for its classic *tascas* and has a pair of fine museums (see p072).

CENTRO/LAS LETRAS/AUSTRIAS

Half-moon-shaped Puerta del Sol is the city's geographical centre and a favoured meeting point. Close by, the magnificent Plaza Mayor testifies to the might of Spain's former empire. Boho Las Letras is steeped in literary history, and Plaza del Ángel and the lanes leading off it are great for tapas.

LAVAPIÉS

Jean Nouvel's bulbous red extension to the Museo Nacional Reina Sofía (see p026) is the gateway to Lavapiés, a working-class area that is starting to gentrify. These days, Calle del Dr Fourquet is the nexus of an arts district of cutting-edge galleries (see p065). You'll also find many specialist bookshops.

LA LATINA

The charming Plaza de la Paja attracts the beautiful people on Sundays, when lunch at the likes of Bahiana Club (Calle Conde 4, T 91 541 6563) is the finale to a weekend of cavorting. Around the packed El Rastro market (see p094) are many photography, secondhand and vintage furniture stores.

RECOLETOS/RETIRO

Punctuated by the Apollo, Neptune and Cybele fountains, Paseo del Prado leads past the cultural steeplechase (see p024) of Recoletos, which is named after a 16th-century monastic order. Retiro is mostly residential to the east, but its focal point and raison d'être is the elegant park (see p027), which offers recreation and art.

LANDMARKS
THE SHAPE OF THE CITY SKYLINE

It's likely that your first view of Madrid will be the vaults of Barajas Airport (see p075). It is a fine welcome to today's Spain. The early-noughties boom found expression in an architectural exuberance, and a crop of striking landmarks were created, including cultural venues such as CaixaForum (see p068) by Herzog & de Meuron, and the vast Matadero Madrid (see p028), a conversion of an old slaughterhouse. Then there are the earlier Torres KIO (see p074), whose audacious appellation, 'Gateway of Europe', started to ring hollow when it was dwarfed by a line of four posturing skyscrapers (see p015) just to the north. As ambitious in its extent is the Madrid Río project. The ring road flanking the Manzanares was sent below ground, enabling 10km of riverside to be reclaimed and landscaped into parks, plazas, foot bridges, a 'beach', and leisure facilities.

Madrid's ancient gems – the majestic 400-year-old Plaza Mayor, the mid 18th-century Palacio Real (Calle de Bailén, T 91 454 8700), which has more than 3,000 rooms – and the grand, austere facades of its urban expansion, in Salamanca for example, were bankrolled by imperial gold and silver pouring in from Latin America. The Gran Vía artery is lined with ornate styles that heralded the 20th century, like the emblematic Edificio Metrópolis (Calle de Alcalá 39), a 1911 Beaux Arts confection topped by a dome and a winged statue; this east-west axis was spruced up and partly pedestrianised in 2018. *For full addresses, see Resources.*

Torres Blancas

Architect Francisco Javier Sáenz de Oiza made his name in the 1950s with a series of sober Miesian row houses in Entrevías. By 1968, when Torres Blancas was unveiled, he had become a whole lot more daring. This 81m-tall apartment complex may not honour its name – it was meant to be two white towers, but the council's reticence and budget restrictions left it as one, raw concrete high-rise – but it remains the city's most desirable address for design aficionados. Sáenz de Oiza's tree-trunk concept melds organic and brutalist styles, and huge pod-like living rooms and circular terraces sprout irregularly from bulbous columns like funghi. If you can wangle an invitation from a resident, you will see the flats are as curvaceous on the inside, and there's an undulating pool on the roof.
Avenida de América 37

Edificio España

This neo-baroque giant has a commanding presence. Brothers Julián and José María Otamendi's 'vertical city' opened in 1953, comprising apartments, offices, retail and a hotel. A haunt of high society, it became notorious for the scandals of the rich and famous and hedonistic parties around its rooftop pool. Its stepped blocks of concrete and limestone rise up 117m, with a facade partly clad in red brick and tiers bristling with white obelisks. It had lain empty since the mid-noughties – an emblem of Spain's property crisis. A Chinese firm bought it in 2014 but authorities quashed proposals to demolish it and build a replica, and it was sold to the Riu group three years later, who are renovating it into a hotel for 2019. Next door, the 142m Torre de Madrid (see p018), finished in 1957, is also an Otamendi design.
Calle de la Princesa 19

Estación de Atocha

Madrid's main train station has always had a fabulous architectural pedigree – among those to work on the 1892 reconstruction (it was built in 1851) was Gustave Eiffel. In 1992, Rafael Moneo's overhaul created a terminal for the then-new AVE super-fast long-distance service (see p096), and one for regional lines, and turned the original concourse, under a soaring atrium, into an indoor public square and botanical garden.

The extension was concealed at the rear to avoid stealing any thunder, yet it quietly does – slender pillars support a huge roof canopy crisscrossed by skylights. However, Atocha's facade (above) remains majestic, with its iron vaults and red stone and brick pavilions. An 11m-high hollow glass cylinder inscribed with messages placed at the site honours the victims of the 2004 bombings. *Plaza del Emperador Carlos V*

Torre Picasso

Finished in 1988, this was the city's big daddy for three decades. Designed by Minoru Yamasaki, architect of the World Trade Center in New York, Torre Picasso has a troubled history of its own – work was suspended in 1984 when the client, an explosives company, suffered financial meltdown and then Yamasaki died. His plans were completed by Alas Casariego. The monolith was devised on a rigorous grid and the vertical lines of the windows are echoed in the landscaping of the plaza in front; the entrance is via an arch cut into the two-storey base. It is now part of the property portfolio of billionaire Amancio Ortega, the founder of fashion brand Zara. At 157m, its height was only surpassed by the Cuatro Torres (opposite) as Castellana reached for the sky in the noughties.
Plaza de Pablo Ruiz Picasso

Cuatro Torres

The city skyline skewed northwards when this quartet was constructed from 2004 to 2009 on Real Madrid's former training ground. At 249m, Pelli Clarke Pelli's sharp-angled Torre Cristal (centre, right), which gets its name from its reflective glazing, is the tallest building in Spain. But only by 70cm from Torre Cepsa (far left), a stacked-box profile by Foster + Partners. Local firm Carlos Rubio and Enrique Álvarez-Sala's 236m Torre PwC (centre, left) has a double skin around three fissured sections, and Henry N Cobb's twisted Torre Espacio, the fourth highest structure in the country, completes the ensemble. Part of a grand plan scuppered by the crisis, the group is a little stranded, although a fifth high-rise, by Fenwick Iribarren and Serrano-Suñer, is due in 2020 (together with a rebranding). *Paseo de la Castellana*

HOTELS

WHERE TO STAY AND WHICH ROOMS TO BOOK

For eons, the belle époque Hotel Ritz (under restoration until late 2019) and The Westin Palace (Plaza de las Cortes 7, T 91 360 8000) were the only choices for fat cats and celebs. However, in the last decade, stately 19th-century *palacetes* have been spruced up with contemporary interiors that contrast with their classical facades. Único (see p022) was followed by Urso (Calle de Mejía Lequerica 8, T 91 444 4458), which melds original stained glass and a modernista lift with a new iroko wood basement spa, The Principal (see p020), Tótem (opposite) and the Palacio de Los Duques (Cuesta de Santo Domingo 5 y 7, T 91 541 6700), with its beautiful, tranquil garden in the heart of Austrias, and a bijou rooftop pool. Recently, there has been a flurry of activity (and a serious amount of extra rooms) around a revitalised Plaza de España – first it was the conversion of Torre de Madrid (see p018), then architects b720 designed the VP (Plaza de España 5, T 91 595 5510) from the ground up, and next comes a revival of the behemoth Edificio España (see p011).

Increasingly, proprietors are vying to establish their hotels as stand-alone social hotspots and banish the convention that you're only welcome if you have a key card. There's a lively scene on the roof at the ME (see p023), in the *vermutería* at Las Letras (see p044) and at funky Only You (Calle Barquillo 21, T 91 005 2222), where the after-work crowd pack out the walnut-panelled cocktail bar. *For full addresses and room rates, see Resources.*

Tótem

Opened in 2016, this sleek boutique hotel inhabits a former aristocratic residence. Its regal facade, replete with Juliet balconies, fronts an interior by Barcelona-based firm Corium Casa in which period details, such as the spectacular pine-and-wrought-iron staircase, are melded with contemporary furnishings. The 64 rooms have a neutral palette, oak flooring, grey wool sofas and Negro Marquina marble bathrooms, and are variously accented with paintings by Yaya Mur, brass door frames, moody blue walls and chartreuse curtains; book one of the double-aspect Junior Suites (above) located in the corners of the property. The restaurant serves market-driven cuisine, or it's a short stroll to Mexican Punto MX (see p051), as well as Retiro park (see p027). *Calle Hermosilla 23, T 91 426 0035, www.totem-madrid.com*

Barceló Torre de Madrid

Madrid's most feted designer, Jaime Hayon, has created a whimsical, vibrant universe for the Barceló, which opened in nine floors of this emblematic high-rise in 2017. On the buzzy ground floor, the city's beloved bear is clad in stripes and tips its hat (a homage to the theatre district), faces are etched in glass, and there are ceramic diver's helmet lights and a 6m-high drinks cabinet in the bar. Ride the lift to the serene hotel proper (lobby, above), all pastel and berry tones offset by gold, and adorned with painterly photos of Spaniards in regional costume by KlunderBie. The 258 spacious rooms feature Hayon's 'Catch' chairs and 'Monkey' tables; the best have balconies. There are also top vistas from the lofty pool, and the restaurant, which serves fine national and global fare, and a terrific breakfast spread.
Plaza de España 18, T 91 524 2399

Hotel Puerta América

It could well have been a bland conference hotel, but due to a bold, visionary approach by Hoteles Silken (who no longer manage it), Puerta América doubles as a showcase for a coterie of the 21st century's more renowned interior designers. Highlights include Marc Newson's aluminium-fin bar and Christian Liaigre's smart restaurant, both of which are extraordinary common spaces. Jean Nouvel's take on global glam pervades the 12th-floor suites, the rooms by Arata Isozaki and David Chipperfield are monochrome and stylish, and the seamless red pod units by Ron Arad incorporate a bathroom, storage and a circular bed. But the most spectacular reveal is Zaha Hadid's sinuous, all-in-white Space Club (above), surely akin to Superman's glacial retreat. *Avenida de América 41, T 91 744 5400, www.hotelpuertamerica.com*

The Principal

Right in the thick of the action, opposite Edificio Metrópolis (see p009) and Círculo de Bellas Artes, The Principal occupies a 1917 neo-Renaissance pile renovated by Pilar García-Nieto and design studio Luzio. Sixth-floor common areas – reached via a bijou iron lift or the marble staircase that spirals around it – are impressively grand and eclectic, with 1950s sideboards, 1970s lights, a fireplace and Chesterfield-esque sofas. The 76 masculine rooms are mainly done out in grey and black; the Junior Suite (above) comes with a 'BKF' chair, artwork by Albert Coma and a bird's eye view of Gran Vía. Ramón Freixa's Ático (T 91 532 9496) is less formal than his eponymous restaurant (see p022), but has an avant-garde menu. Drink in the cityscape *al aire libre* from the roof, or over a cocktail in La Pergola's glazed terrace (opposite). *Calle Marqués de Valdeiglesias 1, T 91 521 8743, www.theprincipalmadridhotel.com*

Hotel Único

María-José Cabré's striking revamp of this 19th-century villa incorporates baroque and arabesque touches, a 13m-tall Formica and maple sculpture by Jacinto Morós, and the odd art deco flourish, as in the marble-floored library. The 44 rooms reinforce the colour scheme of grey and stone, with warmth provided by dark wood and fabric, and bathrooms fitted out by Jaime Hayon (see p018). Breakfast is served in a sunny conservatory that looks onto a secluded garden, with clipped lawns, jasmine and ivy creepers, and inviting lounge chairs. On a special occasion, book Catalan chef Ramón Freixa's restaurant (above; T 91 781 8262), given a refined update by Alfons Tost and Damián Sánchez in 2017, where there is a hushed reverence for its two Michelin stars. *Calle de Claudio Coello 67, T 91 781 0173, www.unicohotelmadrid.com*

ME Reina Victoria

Once the haunt of matadors and celebrities including Manolete, Ernest Hemingway and Ava Gardner, the Victoria has long been en vogue. Its 1919 exterior looms like a giant wedding cake over the pavement cafés in Plaza de Santa Ana, facing Teatro Español in the epicentre of the literary quarter. The interior has been given a slick reinvention by Keith Hobbs. Out of the 192 rooms, opt for a Chic Suite (above) or the high-up Suite ME, a two-level haven replete with spa. The sceney rooftop is a popular local hangout in summer, and gourmet tapas restaurant/ bar Ana la Santa (T 91 145 0334), run by En Compañia de Lobos (see p050), has a mod-rustic vibe courtesy of Sandra Tarruella. Just outside on the right is the legendary jazz club Café Central (T 91 369 4143). *Plaza de Santa Ana 14, T 91 701 6000, www.melia.com*

24 HOURS

SEE THE BEST OF THE CITY IN JUST ONE DAY

To start the day like a local, grab a *café solo* when you rise and then go for *pincho de tortilla* (Spanish omelette) or *churros con chocolate* at San Ginés (Pasadizo San Ginés 5, T 91 365 6546) around 11am. Beforehand, beat the crush at one of Madrid's trio of world-class art museums. A whizz through the Museo Nacional del Prado (Calle Ruiz de Alarcón 23, T 91 330 2800) is essential – highlights are Velázquez's *Las Meninas*, and the nightmarish *pinturas negras* Goya created after he went deaf. The Reina Sofía (see p026) and Thyssen-Bornemisza (Paseo del Prado 8, T 91 791 1370) should also be on your bucket list. To unwind after this cultural overload, Hammam Al Ándalus (Calle de Atocha 14, T 90 233 3334) is an atmospheric bathhouse above an ancient water cistern in the old Arab quarter, or head to Parque del Buen Retiro (see p027) to picnic and boat on the lake before catching the sunset at Templo de Debod (see p030).

In the evening, a bar and *tapa* crawl in La Latina is de rigueur (the pastime even has its own verb – *latinear*). Include stops at Sala Equis (see p042) and Casa de Granada (Calle del Dr Cortezo 17, T 91 369 3596), for views over El Rastro market (see p084). Flamenco originates from southern Spain, but many of its great exponents perform here. The oldest *tablao* (literally, floorboard) is Corral de la Morería (Calle de la Morería 17, T 91 365 1137), a restaurant/bar founded in 1956 that puts on two shows a night. *For full addresses, see Resources.*

10.00 Misión Café

Nolo Botana and Pablo Caballero ushered in the third wave at popular roastery Hola Coffee (T 91 056 8263) in Lavapiés in 2016 and followed up with Misión in Malasaña two years later. At this more food-focused venue, a tripartite hipster menu of Bread, Bowls and Eggs features sourdough toast and a beetroot and hibiscus granola. But the draw remains the phenomenal coffee, which has a punch that makes everything in life sharper, prepared using a Modbar espresso machine with sleek chrome taps that resemble craft beer pumps and enable precision in pressure and temperature. The spare decor of whitewashed brick and black steel, chairs by Graf Studio and a stepped bench-seating system by Juan Ruiz-Rivas (see p089) is softened by plenty of foliage from local botanical design firm Planthae. *Calle de los Reyes 5, T 91 064 0059*

11.00 Museo Nacional Reina Sofía

The Reina Sofía was unveiled in 1990 in the remodelled San Carlos hospital, designed in the 18th century by José de Hermosilla and Francisco Sabatini. Jean Nouvel's shiny red 2005 extension formed a new enclosed space (above) where you'll find *Brushstroke* by Roy Lichtenstein. Ride one of the glass elevators, devised in conjunction with Ian Ritchie, to the second floor, where Picasso's *Guernica* is the undeniable centrepiece. So many landmarks of Spain's modern artistic canon are here, you could do worse than simply get lost in its warren of corridors. Closed Tuesdays. Afterwards, fuel up on a curtly served *bocadillo de calamares* (fried squid sub) at next-door El Brillante (T 91 528 6966) and dive into the contemporary scene at nearby CaixaForum (see p068). *Calle de Santa Isabel 52, T 91 774 1000, www.museoreinasofia.es*

15.00 **Palacio de Cristal**

The Parque del Buen Retiro, laid out in the early 17th century, was once the preserve of the royal family, but since 1868 has been a leafy refuge at the heart of public life. You will find formal gardens and wilder areas, regal statuary, a boating lake and Ricardo Velázquez Bosco's Crystal Palace (above), created for the 1887 Philippines Exhibition, which showcased Spain's imperial reach by displaying the colony's flora and fauna.

The wrought-iron-and-glass confection is topped by a dainty 22m-high cupola. It has a boxy, Greek-cross plan with a colonnaded portico overlooking a lake. The pavilion is used to exhibit site-specific installations such as 'Memorias Imaginadas' (above), in which coloured circles suggested invisible columns, by Madrid-based Mitsuo Miura. *Paseo República de Cuba, T 91 774 1000, www.museoreinasofia.es*

16.30 Matadero Madrid

Luis Bellido's Arganzuela slaughterhouse, a series of limestone and flint structures scattered over a 165,000 sq m site, was one of early 20th-century Madrid's most significant buildings. It was reborn as a contemporary arts centre in 2007 by a group of local architects, who carefully preserved its integrity and used recycled materials including polycarbonates and galvanised iron. There is always plenty going on throughout the various spaces. Either catch a film in the Cineteca, which was designed by CH+QS; an installation in the old refrigeration room (above); a show in the Central de Diseño; or, on Fridays and Saturdays in the summer, a concert in the courtyard. It has become a lynchpin of the regeneration of the Manzanares (opposite). *Paseo de la Chopera 14, T 91 517 7309, www.mataderomadrid.org*

18.00 Templo de Debod

Around the corner from Plaza de España, on the escarpment that looks out to the Guadarrama mountains, is the arresting sight of a genuine 200BC Egyptian temple. It was given to Spain in return for its help in preserving the ancient relics threatened by the construction of the Aswan Dam in the 1960s. Debod would have been totally submerged. It was dismantled, shipped to Valencia and put on a train to Madrid to be rebuilt in Parque del Oeste, on a symbolic site where once the Cuartel de la Montaña garrison had stood – its siege triggered the Spanish Civil War in 1936. The park opened in 1972, and offers much-needed shade, a rose garden and the Teleférico to Casa de Campo. A temple to the sun god Amun Ra, Debod is aligned East-West, its orientation true to the original, and is popular at dusk. *Calle Ferraz 1*

22.00 Fismuler

Following the success of 2014's smash-hit new-wave Spanish restaurant Tatel (T 91 172 1841), chef Nino Redruello and business partner Patxi Zumárraga opened Fismuler in 2016, adopting a Nordic approach to the cooking. The focus is squarely on seasonal ingredients, and dishes depend entirely on what's available at the market. We ordered the tortilla with anchovies and *piparras* (a pepper from the Basque region), a meaty countryside pâté, and chickpeas sautéed with veal and crayfish. This is slow food at its finest. The venue is a sprawling brick basement with cosy nooks (you might have to rearrange the furniture for access) and communal tables of rough-hewn wood. The farmhouse vibe is wholly apt and seems to teleport you out of the city. Closed Sunday.
Calle Sagasta 29, T 91 827 7581, www.fismuler.com

URBAN LIFE
CAFÉS, RESTAURANTS, BARS AND NIGHTCLUBS

Spanish eating and drinking etiquette is confusing and varies from city to city. In Madrid, you're typically given a free *tapa* (perhaps a plate of cured meat) when you order a drink – not uncomplicated in itself, considering there are at least eight sizes of beer, although most common is the smaller *caña*. Always try the house specialities, which are not free and often listed as *raciones* (sharing dishes) – the bull's tail and grilled courgette at Viuda de Vacas (Calle del Águila 2, T 91 366 5847), snails in Casa Amadeo (Plaza de Cascorro 18, T 91 365 9439), *boquerones* (anchovies) in Cervecería Arganzuela (Calle de Arganzuela 3, T 91 366 8680), *jamón* at Casa González (see p054), cheese at La Carbonera (Calle Bernardo López García 11, T 91 110 0669) and, in winter, *cocido madrileño* (chickpea stew with meat and veg) in Malacatín (Calle Ruda 5, T 91 365 5241). From the tap, sample *vermut* at La Violeta (Calle de Vallehermoso 62, T 667 058 644) or Gran Clavel (see p044). Note that you pay only on leaving.

Alongside these traditions, the city has had a culinary revolution. Gourmet markets like Mercado de San Miguel (Plaza de San Miguel) have flourished, while innovative chefs are pushing boundaries at venues as diverse as Sala de Despiece (see p047), Celso y Manolo (Calle Libertad 1, T 91 531 8079), an institution reborn by a young team, and the two-Michelin-starred Coque (Calle del Marqués del Riscal 11, T 91 604 0202), which pulls off a true gastro journey. *For full addresses, see Resources.*

Café Comercial

On the Glorieta de Bilbao junction is one of the city's oldest cafés, founded in 1887 and remodelled in 1953. It was a haunt of writers, artists and actors, as well as the hoi polloi, with a windowed storefront for serious people-watching and a legendary chess club. After a hiatus, it was reborn in 2017 courtesy of design studio Madrid in Love. They retained the swathes of red-brown marble, dark woods, mirrors and chandeliers downstairs, and injected a new sophistication into the first floor (above), with custom-made lamps and banquettes, Thonet and Gubi chairs, brass finishes and Pierre Frey wallpaper. In the kitchen, Pepe Roch produces treats such as tiger mussels and veal sweetbreads, alongside mainstays including *patatas bravas* and *albóndigas*. *Glorieta de Bilbao 7, T 91 088 2525, www.cafecomercialmadrid.com*

A'barra

The execution of the cuisine and design are equally assured at A'barra, which won a Michelin star soon after opening in 2016. Siblings Silka and Héctor Barrio gave the venue character by cladding it in a riot of pale chestnut wood, although the vibe is more restrained in the restaurant (above), which features angular LED lights (made by Arturo Álvarez) and paintings by Juan Barjola and Antonio Suárez. Executive chef

Juan Antonio Medina oversees exquisite seasonal fare, such as waffle of foie and coconut foam; blue lobster with white wine and *lardo* Joselito; and cut iced toffee and mascarpone. Or pull up a seat at the oval marble Gastronomic Bar (opposite) for a multi-course lunch or dinner tasting menu. There's also a 9,000-bottle wine cellar. *Calle del Pinar 15, T 91 021 0061, www.restauranteabarra.com*

TriCiclo

Three is indeed the magic number here at TriCiclo, where a trio of chefs – Javier Goya, Javier Mayor and David Alfonso – have split the menu into three sections, each of which encompasses starters, mains and desserts. In presentation order only, the first, Del Mercado, revolves around fresh produce, be it scarlet prawns or *cecina de León*; the second, Un Paseo, comprises traditional recipes, such as roast pigeon; and the third, Un Viaje, looks overseas for inspiration. Dishes can be ordered as half- or third-size (naturally) portions, so you can mix and match. The reclaimed wood shutters and doors mounted on the walls, light fittings fashioned from Vietnamese wicker baskets and furniture from antiques markets, give the place a rustic, homely feel. Book ahead.
Calle Santa María 28, T 91 024 4798, www.eltriciclo.es/triciclo

Habanera

This is not Havana. Situated in a brutalist concrete corner of Plaza de Colón, named after Spain's most remunerative explorer, this quasi-Cuban-themed restaurant dwells in contradiction. Its most delicious cocktail is called 'No Es Un Mojito', the revelatory *croquetas* are labelled 'not fried', which to the Spanish ear is like 'unroasted roast beef', and its decor is based on a colonial ideal that never existed. Two sprawling floors are linked by a photogenic staircase under an 8m-high atrium. Hanging plants, palm fronds, iron trellises, huge lanterns and several bars break up the space. From the kitchen, visible through the aquarium, chefs prepare a globetrotting menu that visits the Med, South America and Japan. There's live Cuban music on Wednesdays.
Calle de Génova 28, T 91 737 2017, www.habaneramadrid.com

Luzi Bombón

After the success of Bar Tomate (T 91 702 3870), Barcelona-based Grupo Tragaluz followed it up with this more formal and spacious brasserie in the financial district. Sandra Tarruella converted an old bank building using a muted palette, concrete, marble, wood, 1950s-inspired chairs and plump soft furnishings, and custom-made, polished-brass box lights. In a glass-walled kitchen, many of the dishes – sirloin with Padrón peppers, crispy Peking duck, and octopus with mashed potato, coriander and lime – are prepared on the grill. If you can't secure a reservation, settle in to the lounge and order some oysters and spider crab from the raw bar, along with a bottle of rosé cava. A DJ keeps the vibe lively until 2am on Thursdays, Fridays and Saturdays. *Paseo de la Castellana 35, T 91 702 2736, www.grupotragaluz.com*

Casa Mono

Injecting a much-needed dose of fun into commercially minded Argüelles in 2012, Casa Mono has an ornate, turquoise-hued iron facade, and a similarly retro-inspired interior. In the main room (above), Lázaro Rosa-Violán has clad the walls in green and white tiles, and hung giant iron and glass globe pendants. At the mezzanine gin bar, bedecked with mismatched furniture, you can choose from more than 40 labels, but beware, its mirrored ceiling festooned with bare light bulbs can be quite disorientating after one too many. The menu spans global bistro fare and modern takes on national classics – try the *huevos rotos con patata y jamón de Bellota* (the Spanish love 'broken eggs' for lunch or dinner). It stays open late but is buzziest with the after-work crowd. *Calle Tutor 37, T 91 452 9552, www.casamonomadrid.com*

Dstage

Basque chef Diego Guerrero earned two
Michelin stars at El Club Allard (T 91 559
0939) and, since striking out alone in 2014,
wasted no time collecting another couple
at Dstage. In contrast to the OTT interiors
often found in Madrid, the venue is pared
back. The two floors of exposed brick, iron
and concrete, with bare ceiling ducts and
industrial lighting, centre around a skylit
atrium where potted herbs for the kitchen
hang on a system of pulleys; the furniture
was made-to-measure by a local carpenter.
Guerrero is known as one of the country's
most exciting talents, and creations here
have included hare tacos and purple garlic
dessert. There is not an à la carte option;
simply three tasting menus of 12, 14 or 17
courses, which are brought to your table by
the chefs themselves. Book in advance as
there is only space for 40 at each sitting.
Calle de Regueros 8, T 91 702 1586,
www.dstageconcept.com

Sala Equis

In a 1913 newspaper office and printers, which by the mid-1980s had morphed into an adult cinema, closed in 2015, Sala Equis ('X Room') has been converted by local firm Plantea into a brilliantly quirky social hub that retains a rather shambolic air. The ivy-filled Plaza (above) hosts gigs and events and projects visuals above a bar serving tapas, beer, cocktails and G&Ts that stays open late and has a clubby vibe. A skylight has banished movie-theatre gloom, the 1941 art deco-style plasterwork has been kept, mirrored in a neon installation, and seating is on deckchairs, loungers, swings and bleachers. There's also an intimate 55-seat arthouse cinema upholstered top to toe in red velvet, and a smart restaurant and design store, El Imparcial (T 91 795 8986), with interiors by Madrid in Love. *Calle Duque de Alba 4, www.salaequis.es*

La Vaquería Montañesa

Carlos and Pablo Zamora's 'The Mountain Dairy' is all about provenance: sourcing is impeccable, sustainable and organic. The baby goat is reared by Rafael de Bejes in the Picos de Europa, lamb is from Arribes de Duero national park and fish is brought daily from Santander market. The brothers have a fine pedigree – they run institutions Taberna La Carmencita (T 91 531 0911) and Celso y Manolo (see p032). Here, signatures such as five tomato salad with La Jarradilla cheese and pesto, Laredo anchovies with twice-roasted peppers, and steak tartare in bourbon are superb. They are served on rustic ceramics that add colour to the decor of Artek tables, lighting by the Bouroullec brothers, and black and white portraits by Pablo and his mother, María Gorbeña.
Calle Blanca de Navarra 8, T 91 138 7106, www.lavaqueriamontanesa.es

Gran Clavel

At the top of Gran Vía, Hotel Las Letras (see p016) has three classy retro drinking and dining options. At the entrance is a reborn *vermutería*, with stuccoed ceilings, pillars, high tables and a jolly, convivial ambience. Vermouth – aromatic, fortified wine – is a traditional Spanish *aperitivo*, now back en vogue. Try the local Zecchini (rich, dark and fruity) served, as is custom, from the tap. Up a few stairs is the loungey, more refined Bar de Vinos (opposite), where the updated classic dishes, from *ensaladilla rusa* (made with octopus) to the *pringá* (a type of pulled pork) sandwich and *guiso de carrilleras* (pork cheek stew), match the quality of the wine. Expectations ramp up a notch in the formal restaurant (above), where the tripe stew is rightly famed. *Gran Vía 11, T 91 524 2305, www.granclavel.com*

Barra M

Peruvian chef Omar Malpartida first took Madrid by storm with Tiradito & Pisco Bar (T 91 541 7876) and *sanguchería* Chambí (T 603 406 416). At Barra M (pronounced 'Eme'), he reinterprets global street food through a strong native filter, in flavourful combos such as gyozas filled with chicken, yellow chilli, almonds and parmesan; soft-shell crab tempura with steamed Chinese buns; and avocado with roasted prawns, chipotle, *causa*, *cancha*, yuca crackers and corn tortillas. Pisco Sours are also given an international twist, perhaps mixed with Szechuan pepper. The interior is all sharp edges, brushed metal, polycarbonate walls and hard furniture – many of the dishes are prepared at the elongated M-shaped table (above) that gives the place its name. *Calle Libertad 5, T 91 668 4678, barraeme.pacificogrupo.com*

Sala de Despiece

Launched in 2013, the 'Cutting Room' is an exercise in avant-garde dining. The mantra of co-owner Javier Bonet is 'products first and last' and his restaurant, designed in collaboration with OHLAD, appears more like a market stall. Butcher's utensils and colourful polystyrene cool boxes are dotted around; there's a 10m-long polyethylene counter; and delivery-note-style menus detail ingredients, preparation method, origin, weight and price. Innovative tapas, such as fried mangetout with toyomansi sauce and shichimi, or torched truffle with nopal and Mexican adobo, is presented in greaseproof paper and on metal trays. It's first come, first served, although groups of 12 can book. The nearby Museo Sorolla (T 91 310 1584) and its garden is a must. *Calle de Ponzano 11, T 91 752 6106, www.saladedespiece.com*

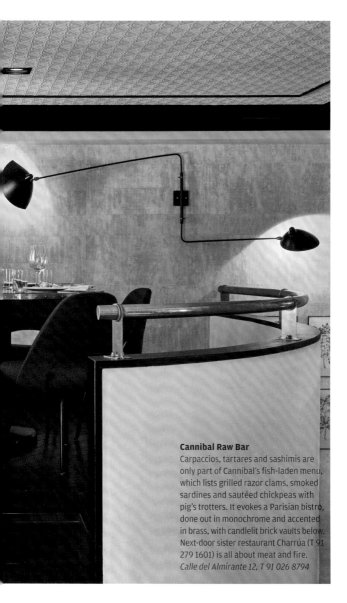

Cannibal Raw Bar
Carpaccios, tartares and sashimis are only part of Cannibal's fish-laden menu, which lists grilled razor clams, smoked sardines and sautéed chickpeas with pig's trotters. It evokes a Parisian bistro, done out in monochrome and accented in brass, with candlelit brick vaults below. Next-door sister restaurant Charrúa (T 91 279 1601) is all about meat and fire.
Calle del Almirante 12, T 91 026 8794

Bosco de Lobos

In the middle of lively Chueca, Bosco de Lobos is a tranquil oasis in the landscaped garden of the Colegio de Arquitectos. Apart from its 1794 facade and a baroque church, the former convent had been destroyed by fire in 1996. Architecture professor Gonzalo Moure incorporated both, as well as sports facilities, a music school and more, into his 2012 intervention. Within a glass-box annex wrapped in a precast cement lattice, this restaurant/bar, with double-height ceilings on the perimeter, was designed by Sandra Tarruella. The action revolves around the square bar, where chefs prepare tapas and Italian comfort food, like fried artichokes, and bresaola, fig and black garlic pizza. The lounge is stocked with architecture books, and there is also a lovely shaded terrace.
Calle Hortaleza 63, T 91 524 9464,
www.encompaniadelobos.com

Punto MX

Chef Roberto Ruiz's Punto MX became the first Mexican restaurant in Europe to win a Michelin star in 2015. The guacamole is prepared tableside with pestle and mortar, tacos come filled with red tuna or Wagyu beef, and the grilled marrow is served in the bone, to be scooped out and wrapped in organic tortillas. It can be difficult to secure a table in the basement restaurant, but the Mezcal Lab (above) offers informal dining and plenty of the strong stuff. The venue is characterised by its tiled floors, sourced from Morocco; other nice touches include Utendi's tree-like coat stands with USB ports, the vintage mirror collection and the Mexican pinks and pulque green in the upholstery. Open 1.30pm to 3.30pm and 9pm to 11.30pm, Tuesday to Saturday. *Calle del General Pardiñas 40, T 91 402 2226, www.puntomx.es*

Platea

Located just off Plaza de Colón (see p073), the old Carlos III cinema was transformed into a foodie's paradise in 2014. The first floor is the domain of headline chef Ricard Camarena (see p098), whose Canalla Bistro champions seasonal produce in a fusion menu. Elsewhere, there's Mediterranean and global fare in the basement; the patio has a selection of concept tapas bars and a *vermutería*, for that pre-lunch ritual; and El Palco, on the second level, is perfect for a *digestivo*. Architect Luis Gutiérrez Soto's 1950s pleasure palace has been superbly renovated by Lázaro Rosa-Violán, and the series of balconies around a deep well are nicely set up for people-watching – and to see the DJs and occasional gigs on stage. Open until 2.30am Thursday to Saturday. *Calle Goya 5-7, T 91 577 0025, www.plateamadrid.com*

Hojaldrería

Javier Bonet (see p047) is a major fixture in the city's culinary landscape, because he's not afraid to experiment. For instance, he mutated Muta (T 91 764 7128) from a place specialising in Brazilian cuisine to dishes from northern Spain, then the Balearics, a smokehouse and an Italian. At Hojaldrería, launched in 2017, Bonet and chef Estela Gutiérrez Fernández's oddball (yet winning) concept is a menu based on puff pastry, divided into 'breakfast, sweet and salty'. Doubters were won over with a decadent beef Wellington burger with egg yolk, foie gras and truffle; it later came with spinach, bacon and duxelles. Of course, the desserts are simply fantastic. Behind a Rococo-style facade, the ex-*mantequería* (butter shop) is as pastel- and sugar-hued as you'd expect. *Calle Virgen de los Peligros 8, T 91 059 9153, www.hojaldreria.com*

INSIDERS' GUIDE

MIRANDA MAKAROFF & PASCAL MOSCHENI, ARTIST AND DJ

Originally from Barcelona and Auckland respectively, artist Miranda Makaroff and DJ Pascal Moscheni settled in Madrid a decade ago, and live in Tirso de Molina. 'We love the ease of improvising a plan here, most places are within walking distance, and there is a sense of social equality,' says Moscheni. 'We don't go to high-end venues.'

They like to rise early ('the sun will probably be shining, it is most days') and check out an exhibition, perhaps at Fundación Mapfre (Paseo de Recoletos 23, T 91 581 6100) or Fundación Loewe (Calle Goya 4, T 91 204 1300). They might have lunch on the 'amazing terrace behind the Prado' at Murillo Café (Calle Ruiz de Alarcón 27, T 91 369 3689) or with friends in Retiro park (see p027) after picking up provisions at Mercado Antón Martín (Calle de Santa Isabel 5, T 91 369 0620): 'We like its authenticity. And the sushi bar.'

In the evening, they often head for tapas at informal, traditional haunts like Casa González (Calle del León 12, T 91 429 5618), Casa Alberto (Calle de las Huertas 18, T 91 429 9356), which is 'almost 200 years old – it's a full-on experience', and La Esperanza (Calle de la Torrecilla del Leal 3, T 91 528 2542), 'for Spanish cuisine from all the regions, made with their signature'. Later on, they suggest 'intimate' Ballesta Club (Calle de la Ballesta 12), which has locals on the decks. To escape, the pair drive an hour into the mountains to Navacerrada. 'In spring, we enjoy the lake. In winter, we ski.'

For full addresses, see Resources.

ART AND DESIGN
GALLERIES, STUDIOS AND PUBLIC SPACES

After 36 years of dictatorship, the abolition of censorship in 1977 heralded an era of artistic expression, and La Movida Madrileña saw an explosion of creativity. Yet the country already had a great legacy, thanks to centuries of royals courting painters, who in turn inspired the pillars of the modern and contemporary Madrid art world, from the cubist Juan Gris to sculptor Juan Muñoz and new realist painter Antonio López, and its three municipal galleries (see p024) are unmissable. But you'll also find CaixaForum (see p068), Museo Sorolla (Paseo del General Martínez Campos 37, T 91 310 1584), the former home of impressionist Joaquín Sorolla, and the Real Academia de Bellas Artes (Calle de Alcalá 13, T 91 524 0864), whose 13 Goya paintings would be a top attraction in any other city.

The financial crisis hit the country hard, but led to a refocus on resourcefulness and innovation, in what many are identifying as a second Movida Madrileña. Within a supportive political climate, a youthful avant-garde is electrifying the scene, opening studios and galleries, and making waves in film, music and theatre. In design, a sustainable approach is exemplified by Álvaro Catalán de Ocón (see p062), best-known for his global 'PET Lamp' series that recycles plastic bottles, Studio La Cube (www.studiolacube.com), whose Project BB fuses lighting and construction debris, and Jorge Penadés (see p061), who makes conceptual furniture from industrial waste. *For full addresses, see Resources.*

Travesía Cuatro

Named after its original address round the corner, where it launched in 2003, Travesía Cuatro now occupies a former mechanics' garage, its painted folding doors forming a pretty facade, with interior patios perfect for launches. Founders Silvia Ortiz and Inés López-Quesada champion young and mid-career artists and are known for forging strong links between Latin America and Europe. In 2013, they established a sister outpost in Guadalajara in a 1929 property designed by Luis Barragán, and represent a number of Mexicans here, including Milena Muzquiz, whose show 'In The Morning, In The Evening' (above) featured characterful ceramics and paintings. Those on the books with strong ties to Madrid are Sara Ramo, Teresa Soler and Asunción Molinos Gordo. *Calle San Mateo 16, T 91 310 0098, www.travesiacuatro.com*

Muros Tabacalera

During nine days in May 2014, the 10m-high perimeter walls of the Tabacalera, a tobacco factory turned cultural centre, and those down Miguel Servet and Mesón de Paredes, were brought to life by more than 20 artists. Above, from left, are panels by Suso33 (see p070), Pincho, Chylo and Rosh333, while local-gone-global Gonzalo Borondo, whose large-scale depictions of the human figure are influenced by Goya and Velázquez, created a self-portrait. An initiative of Madrid Street Art Project, the 130m gallery is refreshed every two years, and crowds gather to watch as the murals are worked on live. Not far away, La Casa Encendida (T 90 243 0322) is also worth a visit. It hosts exhibitions, gigs and cinema, and has a café, eco shop and roof terrace.
Glorieta de Embajadores,
www.murostabacalera.com

Experimento

Ana Arana and Enrique Ventosa founded their design office Plutarco in Chamberí in 2015. The idea for Experimento, a gallery, coworking space and creative community, came during Salone del Mobile 2017 when Arana and Ventosa, after a joint show with other Spaniards including Anabella Vivas and Miguel Leiro, realised that national talent often only met up and collaborated overseas. The project is all-encompassing, also dovetailing fashion, performance and cuisine. 'En Bruto' (above) celebrated the unfinished and the uncontrollable, and mixed construction materials, photography and illustration, in work by Eduardo López, Havi Navarro + Federico Lepre, Piece of Cake and Plutarco, who showed a terrazzo made of fragments found on a building site. *Calle Palafox 7, T 636 287 106, www.experimento.design*

Casado Santapau

Gallerists Damián Casado and Concha de Santa Pau focus on minimalist, geometric and conceptual art and sculpture. Their bright locale, from the high ceiling to the resin floor, provides the perfect frame in a one-time stables of a building that dates from 1890, accessed via an original 1920s gate. The impressive roster is typified by Madrid-based Cubans Alexandre Arrechea, a former member of Los Carpinteros who subverts architecture and everyday items, and painter Waldo Balart, a master of light and colour. German Claudia Wieser's 'What Remains' (above) juxtaposed imagery from the 1976 BBC production of *I, Claudius* with mirrors, drawings and a plinth of precious vessels; it was inspired by Bauhaus colour theory and the Promenade Architecturale. *Calle Piamonte 10, T 91 532 0678, www.casadosantapau.com*

Jorge Penadés

A champion of eco design, Jorge Penadés creates furniture from waste materials from the fashion, car, furniture and olive oil industries. The experimental 'Structural Skin' collection is case in point: its 'Side Table No 1' (above) is crafted from leather leftovers and offcuts, moulded with glue made from animal bones, showcasing the potential of tanned animal hide that would otherwise be discarded. The 'Paraphrase' table is made from reclaimed polystyrene packaging, and the 'Détournement' chair from salvaged metal warehouse shelving. Penadés favours detachable or non-fixed components, enabling him to forego nails or screws in favour of buckles and straps. His work is exhibited and sold at Machado-Muñoz (overleaf). To commission bespoke, email to make a studio appointment.
www.jorgepenades.com

Machado-Muñoz

It was not until 2015 that Madrid got its first gallery dedicated to contemporary design, thanks to Gonzalo Machado and Mafalda Muñoz, who brought it into the public domain via a Chamberí salon with a large storefront. In 2018, it moved to a discreet first floor in Chueca that is well worth seeking out for the three-monthly exhibitions of unique pieces by the likes of Swedish-Chilean Anton Alvarez, who focuses on processes, and local Álvaro Catalán de Ocón, whose 'Rayuela' stool/tables and floor covering played with perspective and geometry. Guest shows have featured Aurèlia Muñoz ('Entes y Otras Criaturas', pictured in the original premises), a protagonist of La Nouvelle Tapisserie from the 1960s to the 1990s.
Calle del Almirante 16, T 91 412 0250, www.machadomunoz.com

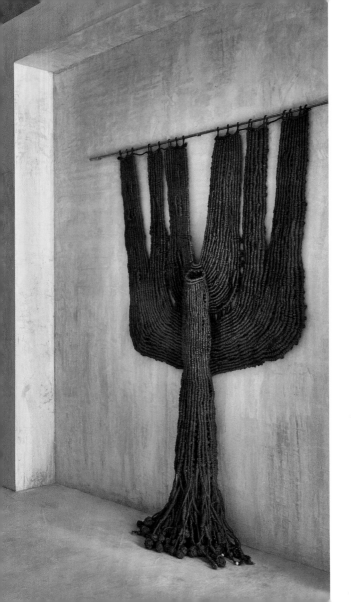

Museo ABC

A relatively recent addition to Madrid's already impressive museum scene, Museo ABC opened in 2010 in the up-and-coming barrio of Conde Duque. It's fair to say that the building itself, a dramatic conversion of a former brewery, is the star. Designed by the Aranguren + Gallegos studio, it has a snowy-white latticed exoskeleton that incorporates the museum, multifunctional areas and restoration workshops, but it is in the café that the architecture reaches its zenith, in a long, light-filled space. The collection focuses on the design and illustration of the *ABC* newspaper and, in effect, traces Spain's modern history, in particular the factionalism during the Civil War, when the traditionally conservative paper was seized by Republicans.
Calle de Amaniel 29-31, T 91 758 8379, www.museoabc.es

Galería Helga de Alvear

German-born Helga de Alvear was one of the first to colonise this street behind the Reina Sofía (see p026), which now teems with galleries. Hers is considered one of the country's most important. She was inspired by the Cuenca and El Paso groups who redefined Spanish art in the postwar period, and began collecting in the 1960s. When she launched her expansive space here back in 1995, she was instrumental in promoting the 'new' artforms of video, photography and installation, which were under-represented at the time. The scope has since widened. Those with a Madrid connection on the roster include political activist Santiago Sierra, painter Prudencio Irazabal ('La Claridad y Lo Incierto', above) and interdisciplinarian José Maldonado. *Calle del Dr Fourquet 12, T 91 468 0506, www.helgadealvear.com*

Galería Juana de Aizpuru

Occupying the first floor of an apartment block in Chueca, this gallery's unassuming facade belies its big reputation. Juana de Aizpuru opened her first venture in Seville in 1970, following up with this location in the capital in 1983. De Aizpuru is renowned for promoting Spanish talent and putting the country on the international map (she founded Madrid fair ARCO in 1982 and the Seville biennial BIACS in 2003). A couple of bright rooms display painting, sculpture, installations, photography and video art. A dynamic stable includes Madrid-based Cristina Lucas, Fernando Sánchez Castillo and Cristina García Rodero, Alicante-born Cristina de Middel and Barcelonian Alicia Framis (three pieces from the group show 'De La Habana Ha Venido Un...', above). *Calle Barquillo 44, T 91 310 5561, www.juanadeaizpuru.es*

Museo de Escultura al Aire Libre

This flyover, supported by graceful pairs of octagonal pillars, was built in 1970 to connect east and west Madrid. And since 1972, the urban space created underneath and around it has provided a setting for 17 abstract sculptures, each by a Spanish artist, created from the 1930s onwards. The crowd-pleasers are Eduardo Chillida's hanging *Lugar de Encuentros III* (above), dubbed the 'Stranded Mermaid', and Joan Miró's bronze *Mère Ubu*, affectionately known as the 'Penguin'. Four decades of exposure to the elements and the touch of countless hands have given the works a weathered feel, and the shadows cast by the bridge, the roar of the traffic, and the sleeping homeless add to the surrealism. This is no sterile gallery experience.
Paseo de la Castellana 40,
www.madrid.es/museoairelibre

CaixaForum
Herzog & de Meuron kept the brick shell of this old power station, topped it with cast iron and added Spain's first vertical garden – leaving a striking impression. You enter via its underbelly, up angular steel stairs to seven floors of concrete and oak galleries, where you might catch a study in reportage photography or an exhibition by painter Miquel Barceló.
Paseo del Prado 36, T 91 330 7300

Suso33

Acknowledged as the undisputed *rey* (king) of graffiti by many of his contemporaries, Suso33 has been tagging the capital ever since 1984, and his trademark *Plasta* paint splodge with one staring eye still peers out from shop shutters today. He crossed into the mainstream in the 1990s as institutions including Reina Sofía (see p026) exhibited his work, and has since branched out into performance art – live painting, often with light and audiovisual technology – in more than 50 cities. Shadowy human silhouettes are also a theme, as seen in this formidable *Presencia* mural on an eight-floor block in Tetuán (Plaza del Poeta Leopoldo de Luis, metro stop Estrecho), part of the council's plan to rejuvenate the barrio in which he grew up. It was created from a crane with a can in each hand over two days in 2013. *www.suso33.com*

Espacio Brut

Furniture designers Braulio Rodríguez and José Cámara set out in El Rastro in 2009 before moving to this more refined gallery space in Chueca in 2013. Their collection features sideboards and shelving systems, predominantly constructed from plywood and oak. They're distinct for their pastel- or bold-toned lacquers and angled legs, which give the pieces a 1950s feel – the elegant cabinets conjure up Bauhaus modernism and Shaker simplicity. Also on sale here is a fine selection of midcentury classics, from German porcelain to teak tableware, Wegner armchairs and Alvar Aalto lights, contemporary ceramics, textiles and art. We were drawn to the 1950s and 1960s Scandinavian crystal and washi paper bags by Japanese firm Siwa. Closed Sundays. *Calle Pelayo 68, T 91 025 8963, www.espaciobrut.com*

ARCHITOUR

A GUIDE TO MADRID'S ICONIC BUILDINGS

Madrid exudes the elegant assurance of a great capital. Boulevards converge at neoclassical fountains; winged lions sit atop the stately Estación de Atocha (see p012) eyeballing frolicking gods on Ricardo Velázquez Bosco's Ministerio de Agricultura (Paseo de la Infanta Isabel 1); and Paseo del Prado, the promenade past the main cultural sites, is shaded by sycamore and magnolia trees. But one of its major historical sights is hidden. Palacio de Liria (Calle de la Princesa 20, T 91 548 1550; visits on Fridays, book in advance) is an 18th-century French-style neoclassical mansion with a superlative art collection.

As for the contemporary, there are not the in-your-face coups of cities like Valencia (see p098), apart from Cuatro Torres (see p015) in the north. There just isn't the space in the ancient centre. And so Madrid has always been stronger at restoring its treasures, from an abbatoir reimagined as an arts hub (see p028) to Centro Escuelas Pías (Calle Tribulete 14), a ruined church that's now a library, and the reborn 1923 art nouveau Cine Doré (Calle de Santa Isabel 3, T 91 369 3225). Brutalists should seek out Torres Blancas (see p010), IPCE (see p076) and the divine Iglesia Nuestra Señora del Rosario de Filipinas (Calle Conde de Peñalver 40). The majority of the city's best modern structures, such as the 1941 Hipódromo de la Zarzuela (see p102), are in the suburbs, but one new-build has just landed right in its core – the Museo de las Colecciones Reales (see p078). *For full addresses, see Resources.*

Torres de Colón

Visionary Madrileño Antonio Lamela's twin towers pioneered suspended architecture in Spain in the late 1960s. A pair of slender concrete pillars supporting cantilevered square roofs were constructed first, and then 20 office storeys clad in brown glass were hung from the top down. The method enabled open-plan floors and the provision of parking spaces in the basement, which would have been otherwise impossible due to the awkward plot. They were finished in 1976, joined at the summit by an art deco-inspired green structure that gave rise to its nickname: '*El Enchufe*' (The Plug). At 116m, they dominate Plaza de Colón – no mean feat in competition with Joaquín Vaquero Turcios' hulking sculptures in the Jardines del Descubrimiento, a towering Columbus statue, and an even larger national flag.
Calle de Génova 31

Puerta de Europa

Philip Johnson and John Burgee's striking 'Gateway of Europe' comprises two of the most easily recognisable skyscrapers in the Madrid cityscape. Completed in 1996, the Torres KIO (they were commissioned by the Kuwait Investment Office and have had various sponsors ever since) rise up 114m and lean in towards each other at 15-degree angles (in a rather amicable manner, it has to be said), making them the first inclined towers in the world. The glittering blocks of granite, steel and glass exude a surreal, sci-fi impression, looming above the workaday offices of Chamartín, and create a dramatic entrance to the city's sparkliest avenue, Paseo de la Castellana. They frame a statue of José Calvo Sotelo, the politician whose murder in 1936 led to the outbreak of the Spanish Civil War.
Plaza de Castilla

Adolfo Suárez Madrid-Barajas Airport
This stunning structure by Richard Rogers and Antonio Lamela (see p073) has a claim to the title of best airport building on the planet. The undulating bamboo awnings of T4 (above), inaugurated in 2006 and renovated in 2013, subliminally shepherd passengers, irrespective of the language they speak, through check-in and boarding using a colour-coding system. Spread over six floors, the terminal is shaded by the overhanging roof, which is punctuated by a series of apertures, enabling natural light to filter through deep 'canyon' shafts to the lowest levels and minimising energy consumption. The luggage-sorting system is impressive too. It requires no handlers and automatically distributes all the cases to the planes from a bomb-proof bunker.
Avenida de la Hispanidad, T 91 321 1000, www.aeropuertomadrid-barajas.com

IPCE

Architects Fernando Higueras and Antonio Miró Valverde's extraordinary Instituto del Patrimonio Cultural de España (IPCE) was unveiled in 1990 in Ciudad Universitaria. Its four storeys of reinforced concrete in a 40m-radius circle envelop an atrium with a glass-and-steel-lattice roof, and its spiky finish led to it being dubbed 'The Crown of Thorns'. Each level is organised into 30 segments (with a break for the entrance) and connected by cantilevered stairs. It is the guardian of national culture, from the arts to architecture, music and bullfighting. Tours are by appointment but exhibitions and concerts, and the sunken library, offer chances to visit. Not far away is another brutalist gem, the Tribunal Constitucional (T 91 550 8000), a 1975 tapered cylinder ringed by honey-tinted windows designed by Antoni Bonet and Francisco G Valdés. *Calle Pintor El Greco 4, T 91 701 7000, ipce.mecd.gob.es*

Museo de las Colecciones Reales

The long gestation period of this museum for the royals' treasure trove has been as much about the handling of public opinion as the construction challenges, due to its sensitive site behind the cathedral. Local firm Mansilla + Tuñón won the tender in 2002, and the exterior is finally complete, although doors do not open until 2020. It is a symbiotic plan that the architects call an 'inhabited retaining wall' – it is built into the south-west corner of the foundations (yet does partially obstruct La Almudena's western face). The rows of granite pillars echo the Ionic columns of the next-door Palacio Real. From within, they frame views of Campo del Moro below. The remains of a 9th-century Muslim settlement discovered during the dig have been integrated into one of the three cavernous display levels.
Calle de Bailén

Teatro Valle-Inclán

Lavapiés, the Jewish ghetto until the end of the 15th century, has long been a magnet for the city's more colourful denizens, like the militant cigarette girls à la *Carmen* and the *manolos* – the lower-class dandies that were such a facet of Madrid in times past. The Teatro Valle-Inclán was charged with revitalising the district when it was built in 2005, yet Lavapiés remains as characterful as ever. However, Paredes Pedrosa's design certainly enlivened the main square and its turn-of-last-century architecture, the boxed volumes making clever use of the triangular footprint and its three-cubed frontage shining at night. By contrast, the interior feels unified thanks to the spare sycamore cladding and floor-to-ceiling windows. The theatre puts on an avant-garde programme of Spanish works.
Plaza Lavapiés, T 91 505 8801, cdn.mcu.es

SHOPS

THE BEST RETAIL THERAPY AND WHAT TO BUY

Slick Salamanca is ground zero for fashion. You'll find the flagships of national brands like Casa Loewe (see p082); the showrooms of small labels such as Malababa (opposite), which sells leather goods, and Aristocrazy (Calle de Serrano 42, T 91 764 9548), for jewellery; boutiques offering global selections, typified by Ambrosia (Calle de Claudio Coello 21, T 91 737 8383); as well as interiors outlets along Calle Castelló, where LA Studio (No 8, T 91 365 7566) is a warehouse of modern and contemporary international furniture.

Malasaña has an indie vibe, with one-offs like Kikekeller (see p095), and a proliferation of concept stores since the pioneering Rughara (see p090). Now, 44 Store (Calle de Valverde 44, T 91 522 7179) is a lifestyle emporium and hair stylist, and El Paracaidista (Calle de la Palma 10, T 91 445 1913) carries multiple designers (look for Isalda's architectural leather bags) over four floors of a former factory, with eateries and bars at the top. Also seek out sustainable style at Ecoalf (see p092), and local menswear guru García Madrid (Corredera Baja de San Pablo 26, T 91 522 0521).

Among the gems in Las Letras are the ceramics atelier Bureau Mad (see p085), the gourmet deli Real Fábrica Española (Calle de Cervantes 9, T 91 125 2021), which proffers Spanish produce only, and some delightful stalwarts including the brilliant Casa Seseña (Calle de la Cruz 23, T 91 531 6840), famous for its capes since 1901. *For full addresses, see Resources.*

Malababa

Among the swanky boutiques on Calle de Serrano, seek out this hip, leather-focused accessories label designed by Ana Carrasco and made in Spain. Key items are the wood-heeled, vibrantly hued 'Paloma' shoes and origami-style 'Knot' clutch, but there are also belts, wallets, hats, scarves, jewellery and shades. Interiors firm Ciszak Dalmas, in conjunction with architects Matteo Ferrari, have reflected the ethos of the brand in the store. Walls are clad in Almerian marble and rough-combed pinky Galician clay, and display units are made of limestone and brass and covered in hide or inlaid with the agate crystals that stud the 'Minihontas' and 'Nanohontas' bags. A curtain artwork by Malababa master craftsman Osvaldo Ruben Thomas shows the artisans' talent. *Calle de Serrano 8, T 91 833 8524, www.malababa.com*

Casa Loewe

Founded in 1846 in Madrid by a group of leatherworkers, the firm is named after a German, Enrique Loewe, who joined in 1876. It went on to become a favourite of Spanish royalty. This flagship store in a 19th-century townhouse has 1,000 sq m of Campaspero limestone flooring, walls adorned with ceramics by Gloria García Lorca, great-niece of the legendary poet Federico, and art by Edmund de Waal and Sir Howard Hodgkin. With Brit Jonathan Anderson as creative director since 2013, the brand has reconnected with its roots, and bright, playful details – leather shirt collars, oversized suede bermuda shorts and belted dresses – often nod towards its heritage. Bags remain a priority: the multifaceted 'Puzzle' has been a big hit. *Calle de Serrano 34, T 91 577 6056, www.loewe.com*

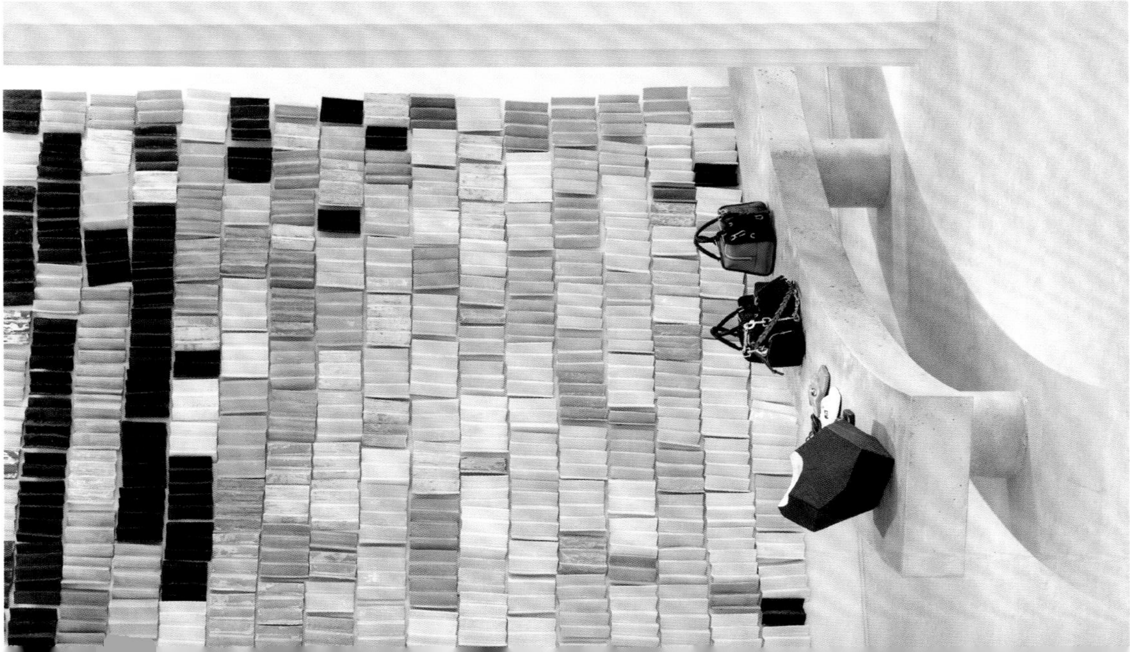

Tiempos Modernos

Founded by Carmen Palacios back in 1988, Tiempos Modernos' two floors are a trove of 20th-century furniture, lamps, porcelain, glassware and decorative objects. You may uncover a modernist classic like Mies van der Rohe's 'Brno' chair, a Prouvé desk or an Eames rocker. It specialises in art deco and pieces from the 1950s to the 1980s, but also champions contemporary Madrid designers (Francisco Gálvez's ceramics) and artists including Blanca Muñoz, José Manuel Ballester and Eduardo Arroyo, and there's a sculpture by local Mar Solís in the courtyard. There are more vintage finds in the antiques stores surrounding El Rastro market – try IKB 191 (T 91 825 9591) for its Almodóvar-esque vibes, while Marantikk (T 91 365 7545) majors in funky lighting. *Calle de Arrieta 17, T 91 542 8594, www.tiempos-modernos.com*

Bureau Mad

Candela Madaria's inviting ceramics store and atelier, in an old dairy with thick stone arches, brims with an impressive range of plates, bowls, cups, tableware and a few indefinables. Influences run from Oriental to rustic (she was inspired to set up the venture in 2016 after studying traditional Spanish techniques). Many of the pieces are created in the workshop out back by a rolling group of 12 artisans. Madaria is the central figure in all this, promulgating the scene all over the country. She takes on makers in rural villages and throws them together with contemporary capital-based ceramicists, such as Jaime Barrutia, Álvaro Villamañán and Begoña Galicia, knowing that they will bounce off each other. There are regular classes and private lessons too. *Calle de San Pedro 8, T 91 052 0941, www.bureaumad.com*

Bastien

Purveyor of cutting-edge streetwear, this compact concept store (two windows wide) is right at home in Malasaña. Its laidback, grungy aesthetic has developed organically since 2016; the exposed brick and a rusty column are original features of the former metalworks, and fleamarket finds like a distressed leather sofa are added if and when. Owner Sebastien Vito Polet curates an edit of global urban labels including Good Worth & Co, Pleasures and Rip N Dip from the States, Berlin unisex brand Atelier About, hats by Betón Ciré, plus jewellery, and fragrances by Mad et Len. Bastien also hosts events, such as a book launch for street-fashion snapper Adam Katz Sinding (AKA Le 21ème), and a wall displays art and photography (for sale) by the likes of Diana Kunst and Pascal Moscheni (see p054). *Calle Divino Pastor 14, T 603 444 358*

Paco Pintón / Yellow & Stone

In 2017, Madrid designers Paco Pintón and Ana Díaz Antolín teamed up to launch this black-fronted corner store in Chamberí, but maintain independence at every other level (including online). It is a tiny space, but it has been given personality with art by Sean Mackaoui and furniture by Simone Nicotra (above). Pintón's signature style of 'tropicalism meets minimalism' expresses itself in clean-silhouetted menswear with pops of bright, beachy colour; palm tree or shark motifs (on belts, caps and wallets); and sweatshirts and tees with Americana slogans. Díaz Antolín's womenswear label Yellow & Stone is classic and timeless, and has a boho feel. Her bestsellers include an elaborately patterned waxed-cotton coat inspired by African capulanas and a leather tote bag with circular bamboo handles.
Calle Covarrubias 7, T 661 242 329

Do Design

Lucia Ruiz-Rivas used to live in Helsinki and has channelled that experience into her welcoming concept store, which has a Nordic-influenced palette. Aged beams and bare stone neatly balance an eclectic edit. A number of the pieces, such as the filament bulbs mounted in wood, are by her brother Juan Ruiz-Rivas, who devised the interior; his nearby studio (Calle de los Reyes 5a) is open by appointment. Dotted around, you'll find casual-chic clothing in natural fibres by H+ Hannoh, furniture by Madrileña Laura Uribe and art by locals Marta Botas and Saveria Casaus, and a tiny café in a timber frame created by Monica Villalba. If you're in this absorbing pocket of the city in the late afternoon, pop into leafy Pinkoco (T 91 196 5994) for a drink. *Calle Fernando VI 13, T 91 310 6217, www.dodesign.es*

Rughara

In 2012, when Malasaña was junkies with needles rather than hipsters with skinny jeans – and the country was suffering an epic economic crisis – Vanesa Serrano opened one of the first concept stores in Spain. The classic shopfront is an illusion, as to go inside is to fall down the rabbit hole of her eclectic tastes, from furniture to mens and womenswear, accessories, lifestyle items and jewellery, arranged in enticing displays. She favours limited editions and local brands, such as shoes by Magro Cardona, plexiglass earrings by Papiroga and vegetable-tanned wallets by Café Leather Supply. The marble walls date from the early 1900s. Playing in the background, or occasionally even live, are bands from the underground music scene.
Calle Corredera Alta de San Pablo 1,
T 91 070 3797

Palomo Spain

Since its launch in 2015, Alejandro Gómez Palomo's menswear has been the talk of catwalk shows worldwide. His theatrical collections marry rich fabrics, meticulous tailoring and a sense of humour, as gender demarcations are gleefully ignored. Sequin dresses and off-the-shoulder tops are not intended to be for women (although they have been worn by some very high-profile ladies). Cultural references are also key. A hunting theme for AW18 featured heavy brocades and slashed doublets, evoking Velázquez's portraits of Spanish nobility. And then there were tweeds and tartans, alluding to classic British outdoor dress, accessorised with animal-hide bags – the 'Gazelle' (above) comes with a horn handle. Find select pieces at Ekseption (T 91 577 4353) and The 2nd Room (T 91 086 9847). *www.palomospain.com*

Ecoalf

The simple white walls, upcycled pine and woodchip, slat pillars and poured concrete floors of Javier Goyeneche's sustainable fashion flagship Ecoalf were designed by Lorenzo Castillo. On the street, a mural by Boa Mistura that states: 'In trash we trust' sets the scene, and inside, everything has been given a second life – rails were once roll bars on military jeeps, and mannequins are built out of reconstituted paper. The range of stylish clothing and accessories incorporates anything from tyres (in soles of sneakers) to coffee grounds (yarn); the 'Livorno Long' puffer jacket is made from ocean waste including plastic bottles. As if in an exhibition, jackets hang in iron box frames, draped with salvaged fishing nets used to create the fabric. Closed Sundays.
Calle Hortaleza 116, T 91 737 4108, www.ecoalf.com

La Magdalena de Proust

Although Spain is one of Europe's major vegetable and fruit growers, it is rare to find a shop stocking only organic produce. Capitalising on this surprising gap in the market, Laura Martínez and Néstor Calvo opened La Magdalena de Proust in 2012. Its industrial ceiling pipes and shelving, surfaces of recycled ceramics, fire-engine-red Smeg refrigerators and whitewashed walls give the delicatessen a clinical look, yet the ambience is neighbourhood store through and through. It sells more than 15 types of bread, seasonal produce from the owners' farm, which is located 20km from Madrid, and a wealth of natural products, including everything from cava to detox kits and washing powder. There are also cooking courses promoting healthy eating.
Calle Regueros 8, T 91 467 3311,
www.lamagdalenadeproust.com

Vintage 4P

On Sundays and bank holidays, the chaotic and slightly bonkers El Rastro fleamarket, a jumble of street stalls, sets up around the axis of Calle de la Ribera de Curtidores. The entire area is packed with antiques stores, typified by this two-floor hoard of quirky vintage European furniture and lighting, which focuses on the latter half of the 20th century. The turnover here is high, so it's always worth dropping in. You could pick up a set of black-lacquered Ercol chairs, a 1970s sofa from Sweden or one of owner Juanma Lizana's retro-inspired industrial lights. Other contemporary items on sale are Artefacto's antique plates, cheekily reworked with mash-up designs featuring skeletons or King Kong, and Spanish artist David Martin's cute recycled mini-robots. *Calle del Bastero 4, T 91 366 5515, www.vintage4p.blogspot.com*

Kikekeller

Celia Montoya and Kike Keller have been developing their eccentric retro-futurist furniture and interior design since 2005. They opened this studio/showroom four years later in the hip Triángulo de Ballesta ('Triball'), in an old tailor's workshop with chipped tiles and peeling wallpaper. It's the perfect setting for their signature welded furniture and lighting, from wrought-iron chairs to stools made out of skateboards,

complemented by Ángel Tausia's concrete lamps. It also sells work by guest creators on a two-month basis, such as Madrileños Studio Lacube, Lucas Muñoz, Ignacio del Toro and Rubén Briongos. From Thursday to Saturday, it doubles as a lounge, which has a bar fashioned from a 1970s tractor and a bathroom set in a replica 1920s lift.
Calle Corredera Baja de San Pablo 17,
T 91 522 8767, www.kikekeller.com

ESCAPES

WHERE TO GO IF YOU WANT TO LEAVE TOWN

Slap bang in the centre of Spain, Madrid is the hub of its transport network, so escaping for a change of rhythm is simple. The 350kph AVE train, built as a link to Seville in 1992, now extends across the country. But we suggest you stay closer to home. It's an hour's drive south to pretty Chinchón, where you should try the local *anís* in the galleried 15th- to 17th-century Plaza Mayor. It is 30 minutes on to Aranjuez (or travel here direct on the Tren de la Fresa, sampling the strawberries for which the area is known) and its Palacio Real, the summer residence of the Bourbons, set in magnificent gardens. Another 40 minutes and you reach Toledo, once home to El Greco. In the cathedral is his superb *El Expolio*, and works by many others.

Or head north from the capital, to escape the heat (and get on the pistes) in the Sierra de Guadarrama (see p054), and continue on 45 minutes to Segovia. Its architecture, hewn from sandstone, offers a potted history of Iberia, from its Roman aqueduct to the 16th-century Gothic cathedral. On the way back, stop off at Felipe II's palace-monastery, El Escorial (T 91 890 5903), in San Lorenzo, adorned with tapestries from cartoons by Goya, and paintings by Titian and Ribera. Nearby, in the Valle de Los Caídos, a huge cross heralds Franco's tomb, within a vast brutalist basilica hewn into the hillside. Many Republican prisoners of war died in its construction and the haunting site remains highly divisive and controversial. *For full addresses, see Resources.*

Atrio, Cáceres

The year 1986 was a big one for Cáceres: the Extremadura city (300km from Madrid) became a UNESCO World Heritage site, for its Roman, Islamic, Gothic and Renaissance architecture; and it gained a gastronomic gem in Atrio. In the historic core, chef Toño Pérez and sommelier José Polo enlisted the services of Mansilla + Tuñón (see p078) to create a seamless transition between the bijou hotel and restaurant (above), which has held two Michelin stars since 2004. Pérez showcases regional produce (his 15-course tribute to the Iberian pig includes tuna with sweet potato and pork chin) and Polo's cellar is one of Spain's best. A superb art collection features works by Antonio Saura, Antoni Tàpies and Thomas Demand. Cáceres is a three-hour drive from Madrid. *Plaza de San Mateo 1, T 92 724 2928, www.restauranteatrio.com*

Valencia

Spain's third city has been cultivating an innovative programme of contemporary culture. Ciudad de las Artes y las Ciencias (T 90 210 0031) is a monumental complex on a wide swathe of dry river bed that may well be Valencia-born Santiago Calatrava's greatest work. Suspended walkways over shallow pools and moats connect various buildings conceived in steel and sheathed in gleaming white *trencadís* (a mosaic made up of broken tiles), a method that was also used by Gaudí. One of the centrepieces, the Science Museum (above), has a cascading glass facade and huge metal 'ribs'. While you're in town, dine at Ricard Camarena's Michelin-starred restaurant (T 96 335 5418; opposite), housed in the buzzy arts space Bompas Gens, where the menu is crafted entirely from ingredients sourced from the surrounding farmland and the Med. High-speed trains to and from Madrid are cheap and frequent; it takes one hour 45 minutes.

MUSAC, León

The multicoloured facade of the Museo de Arte Contemporáneo de Castilla y León (MUSAC) is a nod to the stained glass of the Gothic cathedral (the city is packed with historic architecture, notably Gaudí's Casa Botines). This modern institution, however, takes 1989 as a starting point and focuses on the here and now. Its collection of 1,650 often groundbreaking works by almost 400 protagonists is rotated regularly, and exhibitions have included retrospectives on experimental author José Luis Castillejo and the Cuban textile artist Hessie, and a show by Chilean-Australian painter Juan Davila. Mansilla + Tuñón's bold structure employs more than 3,300 pieces of brightly tinted glazing and an irregular and playful floorplan inspired by Roman pavements. *Avenida de los Reyes Leoneses 24, T 98 709 0000, www.musac.es*

Filandón

The García family run the highly regarded O'Pazo (T 91 553 2333) and El Pescador (T 91 402 1290) fish restaurants in Madrid, and this is their bucolic outpost. Designed by Isabel López Vilalta, five dining rooms in a granite *finca*, and a courtyard shaded by maple trees, host up to 550 people a night, yet somehow an air of Zen prevails. Børge Mogensen's beechwood 'J39' chairs and 'Belloch' seating from Santa & Cole are set at Tom Dixon tables. Its speciality is seafood flamed on the grill. Turn the hour's drive north here from central Madrid into a circular architour. On the way, stop off at the 1963 Parroquia de Nuestra Señora de Guadalupe (Calle de Puerto Rico 1) – part brutalist, part organic – and check out the modernist *hipódromo* (A-6 km8) on return. *Carretera Fuencarral-El Pardo, M-612 km1.9, T 91 734 3826, www.filandon.es*

Palacio de San Esteban, Salamanca

Hewn from the honey-hued rock quarried at Villamayor that has earnt Salamanca the nickname the 'Golden City', this 16th-century convent was restored by local architect Fernando Población Iscar, and now houses a 51-room hotel. The original thick sandstone walls and sturdy wooden beams have been preserved and create a serene ambience, and the Turkish bath and outdoor pool up the chill factor. El Monje serves classic Castilian fare such as *ajoblanco* (garlic soup) and *lechón* (roast suckling pig) beneath swooping vaults and outside on the Patio de los Olivos (above). It's a short stroll to the cathedral (actually two ancient churches for the price of one) and bustling market. To get here from the capital, it is around 90 minutes on the AVE. *Arroyo de Santo Domingo 3, T 90 092 5500, www.hospes.com*

NOTES
SKETCHES AND MEMOS

RESOURCES

CITY GUIDE DIRECTORY

A

A'barra 034
Calle del Pinar 15
T 91 021 0061
www.restauranteabarra.com
Closed Sundays

Adolfo Suárez Madrid-Barajas Airport 075
Avenida de la Hispanidad
T 91 321 1000
www.aeropuertomadrid-barajas.com

Ambrosia 080
Calle de Claudio Coello 21
T 91 737 8383
www.ambrosia.es

Ana la Santa 023
ME Reina Victoria
Plaza de Santa Ana 14
T 91 145 0334
www.encompaniadelobos.com/
ana-la-santa

Aristocrazy 080
Calle de Serrano 42
T 91 764 9548
www.aristocrazy.com

Ático 020
6th floor
The Principal
Calle Marqués de Valdeiglesias 1
T 91 532 9496
www.restauranteatico.es

Atrio 097
Plaza de San Mateo 1
Cáceres
T 92 724 2928
www.restauranteatrio.com

B

Ballesta Club 054
Calle de la Ballesta 12

Bar Tomate 038
Calle de Fernando El Santo 26
T 91 702 3870
www.grupotragaluz.com/restaurante/
bar-tomate

Barra M 046
Calle Libertad 5
T 91 668 4678
barraeme.pacificogrupo.com

Bastien 086
Calle Divino Pastor 14
T 603 444 358

Bosco de Lobos 050
Calle Hortaleza 63
T 91 524 9464
www.encompaniadelobos.com/
bosco-de-lobos

El Brillante 026
Plaza del Emperador Carlos V 8
T 91 528 6966
www.barelbrillante.es

Bureau Mad 085
Calle de San Pedro 8
T 91 052 0941
www.bureaumad.com

C

Café Central 023
Plaza del Ángel 10
T 91 369 4143
www.cafecentralmadrid.com

Café Comercial 033
Glorieta de Bilbao 7
T 91 088 2525
www.cafecomercialmadrid.com

HOTELS
ADDRESSES AND ROOM RATES

Atrio 097
Room rates:
double, from €300
Plaza de San Mateo 1
Cáceres
T 92 724 2928
www.restauranteatrio.com/hotel

Barceló Torre de Madrid 018
Room rates:
double, from €230
Plaza de España 18
T 91 524 2399
www.hotelbarcelotorredemadrid.com

Gran Meliá Palacio de Los Duques 016
Room rates:
double, from €320
Cuesta de Santo Domingo 5 y 7
T 91 541 6700
www.melia.com

ME Reina Victoria 023
Room rates:
double, from €200;
Chic Suite, from €450;
Suite ME, from €2,500
Plaza de Santa Ana 14
T 91 701 6000
www.melia.com/es/hoteles/espana/
madrid/me-madrid-reina-victoria

Only You 016
Room rates:
double, from €180
Calle Barquillo 21
T 91 005 2222
www.onlyyouhotels.com

Palacio de San Esteban 103
Room rates:
double, from €150
Arroyo de Santo Domingo 3
Salamanca
T 90 092 5500
*www.hospes.com/salamanca-palacio_*
esteban

The Principal 020
Room rates:
double, from €300;
Junior Suite, from €850
Calle Marqués de Valdeiglesias 1
T 91 521 8743
www.theprincipalmadridhotel.com

Hotel Puerta América 019
Room rates:
double, from €140;
Arata Isozaki rooms, from €140;
David Chipperfield rooms, from €140;
Ron Arad rooms, from €140;
Space Club room by Zaha Hadid,
from €190;
Jean Nouvel suites, from €350
Avenida de América 41
T 91 744 5400
www.hotelpuertamerica.com

Hotel Ritz 016
Room rates:
prices on request
Plaza de la Lealtad 5
T 91 701 6767
www.mandarinoriental.com/madrid

Tótem 017
Room rates:
double, from €150;
Junior Suite, from €230
Calle Hermosilla 23
T 91 426 0035
www.totem-madrid.com

Hotel Único 022
Room rates:
double, from €280
Calle de Claudio Coello 67
T 91 781 0173
www.unicohotelmadrid.com

Urso 016
Room rates:
double, from €200
Calle de Mejía Lequerica 8
T 91 444 4458
www.hotelurso.com

VP Plaza España Design 016
Room rates:
double, from €230
Plaza de España 5
T 91 595 5510
www.plazaespana-hotel.com

The Westin Palace 016
Room rates:
double, from €320
Plaza de las Cortes 7
T 91 360 8000
www.westinpalacemadrid.com

WALLPAPER* CITY GUIDES

Executive Editor
Jeremy Case

Photography Editor
Rebecca Moldenhauer

Art Editor
Jade R Arroyo

Editorial Assistant
Josh Lee

Photo Assistant
Daniëlle Siobhán Mol

Contributors
Alexander Fiske-Harrison
Igor Ramírez García Peralta
Katherine Robinson

Sub-editors
Emma Barton
Marta Bausells
Belle Place
Ed Upright

Intern
Lydia Dunton

Madrid Imprint
First published 2006
Sixth edition 2018

ISBN 978 0 7148 7651 1

More City Guides
www.phaidon.com/travel

Follow us
@wallpaperguides

Contact
wcg@phaidon.com

Original Design
Loran Stosskopf

Map Illustrator
Russell Bell

Production Controller
Gif Jittiwutikarn

**Assistant Production
Controller**
Sarah Scott

Wallpaper* Magazine
161 Marsh Wall
London E14 9AP
contact@wallpaper.com

Wallpaper*® is a
registered trademark
of TI Media

Phaidon Press Limited
Regent's Wharf
All Saints Street
London N1 9PA

Phaidon Press Inc
65 Bleecker Street
New York, NY 10012

All prices and venue
information are correct
at time of going to press,
but are subject to change.

A CIP Catalogue record for
this book is available from
the British Library.

PHOTOGRAPHERS

Phillipe Milton
Madrid city view,
inside front cover
Torres Blancas, p010
Estación de Atocha,
pp012-013
Misión Café, p025
Museo Nacional Reina
Sofía, p026
Templo de Debod, p030
Fismuler, p031
Café Comercial, p033
A'barra, p034, p035
Habanera, p037
Sala Equis, p042
Gran Clavel, p044, p045
Barra M, p046
Sala de Despiece, p047
Cannibal Raw Bar,
pp048-049
Hojaldrería, p053
Miranda Makaroff and
Pascal Moscheni, p055
Travesía Cuatro, p057
Galería Juana de Aizpuru,
p066
CaixaForum, pp068-069
IPCE, p076, p077

Tiempos Modernos, p084
Bureau Mad, p085
Bastien, p086
Paco Pintón / Yellow
& Stone, p087
Do Design, p088, p089
Rughara, p090
Kikekeller, p095

Jesús Alonso
Cuatro Torres, p015
ME Reina Victoria, p023
TriCiclo, p036
Luzi Bombón, p038
Casa Mono, p039
Dstage, pp040-041
Bosco de Lobos, p050
Punto MX, p051
Platea, p052
Muros Tabacalera, p058
Museo de Escultura al
Aire Libre, p067
Suso33, p070
Espacio Brut, p071
Ecoalf, p092
La Magdalena de
Proust, p093
Vintage 4P, p094
Filandón, p102

Luis Asín
Museo de las Colecciones
Reales, p078
Teatro Valle-Inclán, p079

Jordi Bernardô
MUSAC, pp100-101

Ben Blossom
Valencia, p098

Joaquín Cortés
Galería Helga de
Alvear, p065

Brenda Germade
Jorge Penadés, p061

Paco Gómez/NOPHOTO
Matadero Madrid, p029

Alamy
Edificio España, p011
Palacio de Cristal, p027
Torres de Colón, p073
Puerta de Europa,
p074
Adolfo Suárez Madrid-
Barajas Airport, p075

MADRID

A COLOUR-CODED GUIDE TO THE CITY'S HOT 'HOODS

SALAMANCA
This upper-class playground is all luxury boutiques, swanky restaurants and hip hotels

CASTELLANA
A major artery scythes through this northern business district, flanked by office towers

MADRID RÍO
Once-forgotten, now revitalised, the river and its banks have been given over to leisure

CHUECA/MALASAÑA/CONDE DUQUE
The left-field barrio saw the birth of La Movida Madrileña and is still ahead of the curve

CENTRO/LAS LETRAS/AUSTRIAS
Immerse yourself in the grandeur of imperial history in Plaza Mayor and the Palacio Real

LAVAPIÉS
An artistic quarter that is a draw for its contemporary galleries and progressive theatre

LA LATINA
Bar hop along Calle Cava Baja, which is lined with taverns, restaurants and flamenco joints

RECOLETOS/RETIRO
Madrid's cultural enclave of museums and statuary encompasses the stately Retiro park

For a full description of each neighbourhood, see the Introduction.
Featured venues are colour-coded, according to the district in which they are located.